May the Spirit of Alaska
Run Wild in your Heart!

Jimmy Bhell

The Spirit of Alaska

by Jimmy Tohill

Library of Congress Control Number: 2011927651

ISBN: 978-1-57833-602-9

First Printing May, 2011
Second Edition Printing December, 2014

Design and layout - Jimmy Tohill
Photography and poetry - Jimmy Tohill
Final file preparation, review and layout - Vered Mares / Todd Communications

Printed by Samhwa Printing Co., Ltd., Seoul, Korea,
through Alaska Print Brokers, Anchorage, Alaska.

Published in Alaska by Jimmy Tohill / Old Sourdough Studio - Denali

For additional copies contact :
Jimmy and Vicki Tohill / Old Sourdough Studio
P.O. Box 455 Healy, AK 99743
907-683-1011
oss@mtaonline.net
www.oldsourdoughstudio.com
www.thespiritofalaska.com

or stop by Old Sourdough Studio
at the McKinley Chalet Resort - Mile 238.5 Parks Hwy., Denali, AK.

Cover photo: A grizzly bear (*Ursus arctos horribilis*) searches for arctic ground squirrels in their burrows during a fall snowstorm in Denali National Park.

Table of Contents

The Spirit of Alaska

The spirit of this place goes beyond the human race
And tells a tale of times gone by.
From the beauty of the land to the wildness so grand,
The spirit shines bright in the sky.

From the dark winter nights with the dance of the Lights,
The spirit of Alaska whispers quite clear;
To the summer days so long that the spirit sings a song
Of a place that can sooth all fear.

The creatures that roam from Ketchikan to Nome
Have the spirit within their heart
And the weather that rules with its magnificent tools
Makes the creatures humble and smart.

A wolf's lonesome howl, the hoot of a great grey owl;
The spirit of Alaska has a majestical call.
The strength of the brown bear, the feel of the fresh air
Tames man's ego and makes it seem small.

The vastness of its size is quite a surprise
To those that have not seen it before.
The diversity of the land is like the grains of sand
That are scattered from shore to shore.

A bull moose in a pond, a fragile fern frond,
The spirit of Alaska is strong and meek.
There's the Arctic in winter and a volcano's center,
The spirit is quite unique.

Wolverine and minks, there's the elusive wild lynx;
Creatures that can be hard to find.
The mighty killer whale and the polar bear so pale
Are Alaskans that are one of a kind.

The Spirit of Alaska

Salmon return each year and fill the rivers that are here
With a bounty that comes from the sea.
The swans come to nest with the geese and the rest
Of the birds that migrate so free.

The eagles that soar and the rivers that roar
Through the trees and mountains so tall;
The caribou in rut and the Dall sheep that butt;
The spirit has a cycle for all.

Alaska is wild yet innocent as a child
And its spirit is mighty and bold.
It is strong and true and will mesmerize you
If you open up and let it take hold.

The spirit is there to make all aware
That life is a grand thing indeed.
Take a look around and listen to the sound
The spirit has planted its seed.

The seed it will grow into what we should know
To make this life what it can be.
Experience the spirit and you will sure hear it
Sing about life and how to be free.

The soft rolling tundra and the glaciers that thunder
Are the spirit of Alaska's fine art.
The creatures that roam from Ketchikan to Nome
Hold the spirit deep in their heart.

Hold the spirit deep in your heart!

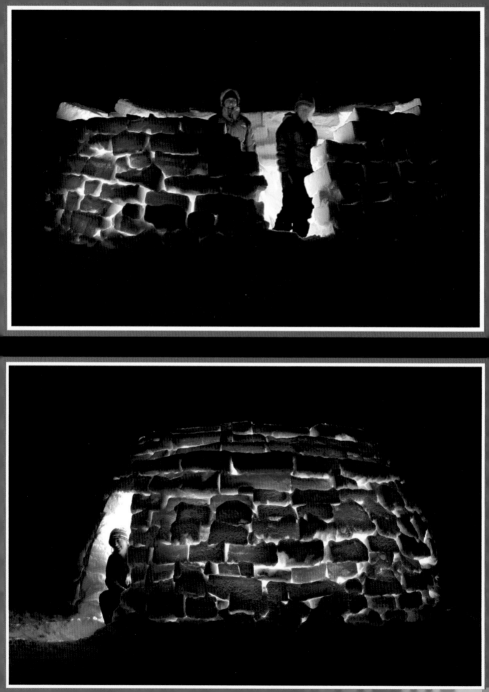

Alaska, Alaska – home of the midnight sun;
I have come to learn and have some fun.
Alaska, Alaska – there's so much land;
Things are so beautiful, life is so grand.
I've climbed on glaciers; I've seen some bears;
I've left my worries; I have no cares;
Except for the cares of life and health.
Alaska, Alaska – has its own special wealth.
The wealth of the eagle, the moon and the sky;
You have to see it with your own gazing eye.
Alaska, Alaska – home of the free;
There's so much here, so much to see.
The Dall sheep, the caribou, the griz, the moose;
Here in Alaska, a man can cut loose.
Cut loose from the impurities of the modern city;
Here in Alaska, things are so pretty.
Alaska, Alaska – I love it already;
Insecurities are gone, I feel so steady.
This is a place everyone should go
To learn the things everyone should know.
Things like wildness, beauty and strength,
Where summer sun is forever – 24 hours in length.
Alaska, Alaska – I think I'll call home;
Where I'll have a life to roam and roam.
Roam through the mountains down to the sea,
Alaska, Alaska – home of the free!

Early Summer in Denali

The grizzly siblings roam the tundra eating
Grasses, roots, old berries from last fall.
The old white ram sits stoic on the ridge
Watching his nine young competitors
Playfully practicing battle with one eye,
And with the other,
Watches his harem and offspring across the valley.

The bull moose heads out alone for lush tundra.
The golden eagle soars high and has his eye on
The newborn offspring of the old white ram.
The marmot whistles and ducks into his burrow.

The caribou lays down on a patch of snow
Seeking relief from biting bugs.
The longtailed jaeger returns, flying low in search of voles.
The wolf, elusive, sees it all.

The Beauty of No Indoor Plumbing

I just went outside to pee
And much to my aglee,
It's thirty below
And the sky is aglow
With northern lights to see.

The northern lights you see
Can help to set you free,
You'll stand and stare
With frozen nose hair
And forget you came out to pee.

If you give the lights a chance,
They'll put you in a trance;
From green to red,
As you lay back your head
And watch their magical dance.

It seems from the end of September
Until I just can't remember,
It gets so darn cold
And the dark gets real old,
But the dance of the lights keeps you limber.

You'll feel so warm inside,
And the smile you just can't hide,
While watching the lights
On cold winter nights,
You really can't beat the ride.

It's a ride so pure and free,
It's a ride you just have to see;
At thirty below
And the sky aglow,
Don't forget you came out to pee.

The Spirit of the Iditarod

Out cruisin' along the Iditarod Trail,
Dogs just a trottin' and waggin' their tail.
They leave civilization and head up the Yentna;
Before they know it they're at the checkpoint at Skwentna.
It's on down the trail and up through the Shell Hills,
Then on to Finger Lake for the start of the thrills.
Down the Happy River steps their brakes dig a groove,
Their eyes on the trail for that critical move.
That critical move they just have to make
If they want to check in at Puntilla Lake.
On into the Alaska Range across Ptarmigan Flats,
Up through the beautiful majesty of Rainy Pass.
Better hold on tight and let out a yell;
It's down through the gorge they call the Dalzell.
Out on the Tatina River to the roadhouse at Rohn;
On across the Farewell burn mushin' alone.
The view of Denali can be very unique;
There's the Buffalo Camp and the cabin at Bear Creek.
If they make it to Nikolai all intact
They've been through the worst and that's a fact.
Out on the trail to the Kuskokwim River,
If the wind is howling it will kick in a shiver.
Into McGrath for one heck of a meal;
The Iditarod race is quite an ordeal.
This is a good place for their 24 hour break,
There is hot water and supplies they can even get cake.
Maybe they'll wait for Takotna's quieter style
Where the teams are greeted with a big local smile.
It's on to Ophir and if they arrive at night
They will check in at Forsgren's by lantern light.
The Aurora can put on an amazing show,
With greens and reds reflecting off the snow.
On to the ghost town of Iditarod on a long lonely ride;
Out in the wilderness of Alaska - mushin' with pride.
Proud to be part of this Last Great Race;
It shines so brightly in each mushers face.

The Spirit of the Iditarod

They leave the old cabin by pullin' the hook
And it's on down the trail to Shageluk.
There's no one around, not a cabin in sight;
Alone with their dogs, the feeling's just right.
Mushin' on to Anvik and the Yukon so grand;
From here to Kaltag they're on the river not land.
Strong winds and cold temps are what the mushers fear,
As it can be quite intimidating for the dogs I hear.
On the mighty Yukon River through Grayling and beyond;
To Eagle Island and Kaltag then southwest to the big pond.
The big pond called the Bering Sea at Unalakleet,
This is a good place to rest and warm their feet.
They mushed over the portage and onto the coast,
From here to Nome can be a challenge for most.
Along the coast and up the Blueberry Hills,
Down to Shaktoolik there can be deadly wind chills.
From here to Koyuk it's out on sea ice;
The weather on Norton Sound can be not very nice.
The wind can kick up with hurricane force;
At subzero temps it shows no remorse.
It can turn back their teams and frostbite their skin,
But the mushers push on in search of that win.
Make it to Elim and there's a bit of a reprieve,
Get out of the wind and the dogs might not leave.
From here to Golovin there's a cabin at Walla Walla,
Then a climb up Little McKinley that will make a musher holler.
On into White Mountain for a mandatory eight;
If they are out in front here then life is just great.
But if there is a storm on the next little jaunt,
The trip to Safety can be one hell of a haunt.
If it's nice weather it can be an enjoyable run,
And on into Nome for the finish and fun.
When under the burled arch there's a team and a sled
With a musher holding on with a high hanging head;
The dogs and the mushers have learned a lot since the start;
Now the Spirit of the Iditarod is etched in their heart!

Cold and Dark

The snow is piling up and the food is getting thin;
Soon all of the bears will be holed up in their den.
The temperature is dropping and the animals all know
That this is the season that is dominated by snow.
Most birds fly south and most people as well;
For many, an Alaskan winter is a living hell.
There are some animals and people that thrive as they should
When the land turns to white and the living is good.
The lynx, the wolf, the snowshoe hare,
The fox, the moose, the caribou all share
The beauty you find in the short winter days;
It's harsh but it's sweet in so many ways.
The hustle of summer is gone with the winds;
Now people have time to share with their friends.
The light might not be long but the quality is there;
The beautiful soft hues you just can't compare.
The solitude, the pureness, the essence of being,
Stick around in the winter and that's what you'll be seeing.
Along with the dance of the northern lights show
You'll experience some things that will sure make you grow.
At forty below you learn to be ready;
It makes you tough, humble and steady.
Just watch the Dall sheep up in the high places;
They're the toughest animals with the most peaceful faces.
The Raven, the magpie and the grey jay
Are three hearty birds that manage to stay.
There's not much food but the competition is thin;
And that alone is a big reason to grin.
People will often ask, "isn't it just cold and dark?"
Look into an Alaskan's eyes and you will see the spark.
The highways are empty but our hearts are full;
The winter in Alaska has a mystical pull.

Cold and Dark

It's a pull that many will never quite see;
It's cold, it's dark but it's ever so free.
Cars don't want to start so you have to plug in;
With the clothes you must wear no one looks thin.
When it gets colder than thirty below,
Cover up good don't let your skin show.
Cause frostbite will get you if you're not prepared;
It's only the foolish that tend to get scared.
If you learn to be wise and know all the tricks,
It's quite enjoyable cruisin' around in the sticks.
There's snow to play in and ice all around;
It's amazing the distance of the travel of sound.
Propane stays liquid at about forty below;
You must heat your tank if you want it to flow.
At these temps you can throw hot water that's wet;
And ice fog and snow is all that you'll get.
The cold it does some very interesting things,
As the aurora dances overhead with its angelic wings.
There is a beauty in the harshness I will have to say;
It's cold and dark and I like it that way.

The River

Walk along the river, take a look around,
Feel the awesome power, listen to the sound.
The pulse of the Earth is what you will hear,
Day in, day out and year to year.
The river is the bloodstream of life as we know it;
Float down the river and it will sure show it.
It will show you the life that abounds on its shore;
The caribou, the grizzly, the wolf and much more.
The spruce, the willows, the alders and such;
The lichens, the mosses - there's just so much.
And then there are those that live on the water,
The Harlequin duck and the rare river otter.
The river it flows and it changes the land,
Carving out canyons, turning rock to sand.
It flows silty in the summer and clear in the fall;
In the middle of winter it doesn't seem to flow at all.
It looks frozen solid at fifty below;
But the river keeps flowing under ice and snow.
The river is persistent, flowing all year;
The river is really what brought me here.
The river it's called Nenana by name;
But this river or that they are all the same.
Same in the sense that they are the bloodstream of Earth;
Carrying away the old and giving new birth.
Helping the cycles of constant change,
Helping the Earth to rearrange.
Change is something that we seem to fear;
But without change we would not be here.
So here's to the river and the changes it brings;
Listen very carefully for the river it sings.
It sings of the Earth and the constant strife
To bring about change that enhances life.
Walk along the river, take a look around,
Feel the awesome power, listen to the sound.

Seasons of the North

The spring in the North means the return of the sun,
Revealing to all what the winter has done.
Fading away those soft winter hues;
The oranges, the pinks, all the different blues.

The sun comes back strong and melts away the snow,
It will soon overpower the aurora's night glow.
The land changes fast from white to green,
Next thing you know, it's a summer scene.
The magical summer of this great north land
Can only be felt if seen first hand.

A grizzly at rest with her cubs running 'round,
A caribou strolls by with his nose to the ground.
Up high in the cliffs the Dall sheep give birth
To little white lambs new to this Earth.

Moose are glad to see the fresh leaves on the trees
As their newborn calves spring about as they please.
The swans, the cranes, the terns and the rest
Have returned once again to feed and to nest.
Wildflowers in bloom with colors so bright,
Daylight so long that there is no night.

Salmon fill the rivers and lakes fill with loons;
White puffy clouds fill the afternoons.
Beavers mend their dams and river otters play,
All the while knowing that the sun won't stay.

Soon it will get dark real early in the morning
And the fireweed will display its end of summer warning.
Termination dust will come to the high peaks;
Moose will be in the rut for several weeks.
The tundra will change from greens to reds;
Dall sheep will begin to butt their heads.

Seasons of the North

Fall is here, it's brief, it's fast;
The Sandhill cranes know it won't last.
They leave in V's of thousands or more,
They're not going to stay for what's in store.

Daylight is dwindling and the ground is white;
The sun's sinking south for a long winter's night.
The bear's holing up in a snow cave somewhere;
The lynx is on the prowl for a snowshoe hare.
Moose are wading through chest deep snow;
The aurora borealis puts on a grand show.

Caribou head for their winter ground;
Wolves follow intensely without a sound.
The Alaskan winter is in its full swing
Until once again, another spring!

The animal I've watched that is the most impressive of all
Is the beautiful white sheep named after a man named Dall.
Most birds fly south and the bears go to sleep;
But high on the ridges you'll find the Dall sheep.
They stick it out through the long winter nights
Under the glow of the wild northern lights.
They live up on the ridges at sixty below
Wading through pockets of chest deep snow.
They dig in the snow looking for left over grasses;
They'll chew lichen off rocks in the high mountain passes.
If they make it through winter, in the spring of the year,
Little white lambs will begin to appear.
Clinging to cliffs to stay away from wolf packs,
Fear of sheer heights this animal sure lacks.
Golden eagles soar the cliffs trying to catch them off guard;
They are alert and agile, they make it quite hard.
The lambs must be quick right from their birth
If they want to grow old here on this earth.
The ewes raise the lambs and the rams hang together;
They hang in the high mountains no matter the weather.
But sometimes they'll come down in search of fresh water,
Always ready to run to avoid the wolves' slaughter.
The big ram is king and he keeps an eye on them all;
He knows where his harem is especially in the fall.
This is when other rams will challenge his reign;
The challenge of head butts is often in vain.
Young rams will practice and butt heads for hours;
The big ram just watches, he realizes his powers.
Mating takes place and the ram he does know
That here comes the cold, the dark and the snow.
The harsh winter winds and the air so pure,
High on the ridges these white sheep endure.

Run Wild

The river full of salmon, bears all around,
Out in the wilds of Alaska, serenity is found.
Blueberries, cranberries wild everywhere;
Pure rivers, soft tundra, freshness in the air.
Walking through moose trails, bear trails and streams;
Here in the wild ... living my dreams.

A caribou stands in a bog by a creek;
You can tell he's wild, he's strong not weak.
Run wild, I say, run wild and free;
Run wild down a river and you will see.
You will see the things that make you grow;
You'll feel the freedom, the wildness will show.
It will show in your heart, you'll feel it throughout,
You'll have a feeling for wildness and what it's about.

Run wild down the rivers, run wild in the hills,
Seek out the pureness, the greatness, the thrills.
From bears feeding on salmon to the eagles that soar
On Alaska's rivers I have found this and much more.
There were ducks and beavers and beautiful blue sky;
There were rapids that roared and a wolf's lonesome cry.
I am so glad there are still places like this,
Where you can feel the touch of nature's sweet kiss.

Index

Index

About the Photographer/Poet

Jimmy Tohill came to Alaska as a river guide and photographer in 1987 from Durango, Colorado. Born and raised in Texas, Tohill longed for the mountains and wild places and followed his heart to Alaska. He and his wife, Vicki, built their log home themselves. They lived in a 12 x 16 cabin with no running water for 6 years while they hand built their home out of pocket. They now live with the comforts of running water in Healy, just 10 miles north of Denali National Park. Jimmy and Vicki have owned and operated Old Sourdough Studio at the McKinley Chalet Resort in Denali since 1998. Old Sourdough Studio is a very unique photography studio with a state of the art digital lab that also specializes in white water rafting photos on the Nenana River.

Along with helping run the studio and building another log cabin Jimmy gets out in wild places throughout Alaska as much as possible and he always has his camera and pen. Tohill says: "I feel fortunate to be able to live in a place where this kind of beauty abounds all around. I really enjoy sharing some of this beauty and the deep feelings that go along with it. Plus, it's just plain good for the soul."

photo by Vicki Tohill